בס"ד
לד׳ הארץ ומלואה

This book belongs to

Please read it to me!

My Shabbos 1,2,3's

By
SURIE FETTMAN

Illustrated by
PATTI NEMEROFF

Hachai PUBLISHING

"To my children, who continually inspire me." S.F.

"To my daughter, Jenni and my father, Mel, who each in their own special ways have enriched my life and taught me so much about giving." P.N.

My Shabbos 123's

First Edition – September 1996 / Elul 5756
Sixth Impression – July 2014 / Tammuz 5774

Copyright © 1995 by **HACHAI PUBLISHING**
ALL RIGHTS RESERVED

Editor: Devorah Leah Rosenfeld
Layout: Eli Designs

ISBN-13: 978-0-922613-61-8
ISBN-10: 0-922613-61-3
LCCN: 96-76744

HACHAI PUBLISHING
Brooklyn, N.Y.
Tel: 718-633-0100 Fax: 718-633-0103
info@hachai.com www.hachai.com

Printed in China

Donny and Dina
are a brother and sister
who like to set the table
before Shabbos.

Donny and Dina
Can count to ten.
As they set the Shabbos table,
Let's count along with them!

One silver cup,
All shiny and bright,

So Father can make Kiddush
On Friday night.

Two fresh challos,
Crisp and yummy,

Donny can't wait
Till they're in his tummy.

Three small bentchers,
We sing out loud with them.

Donny can't read yet,
But he can thank Hashem.

4

Four red roses
For the Shabbos day,

Let's put them in water
Right away!

Five Shabbos candles,
So tall and white,

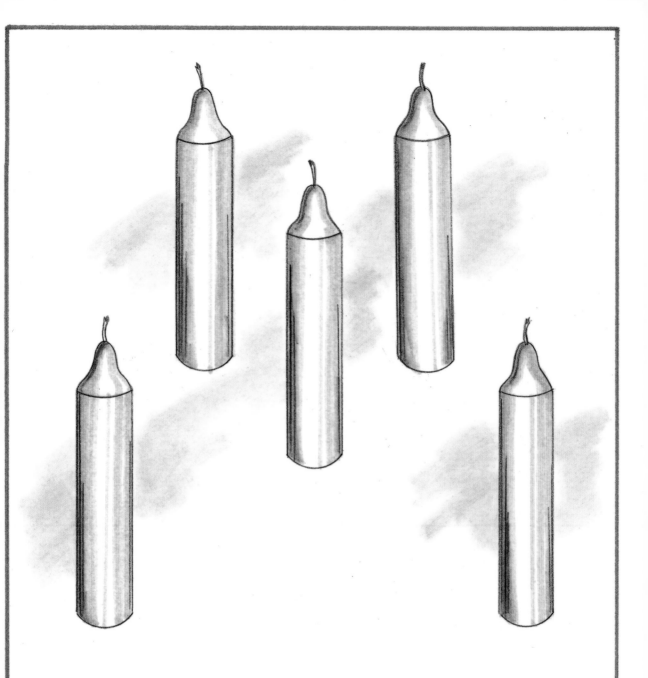

Are ready for Mother
And Dina to light.

Six pretty plates,
Nicer than the rest,

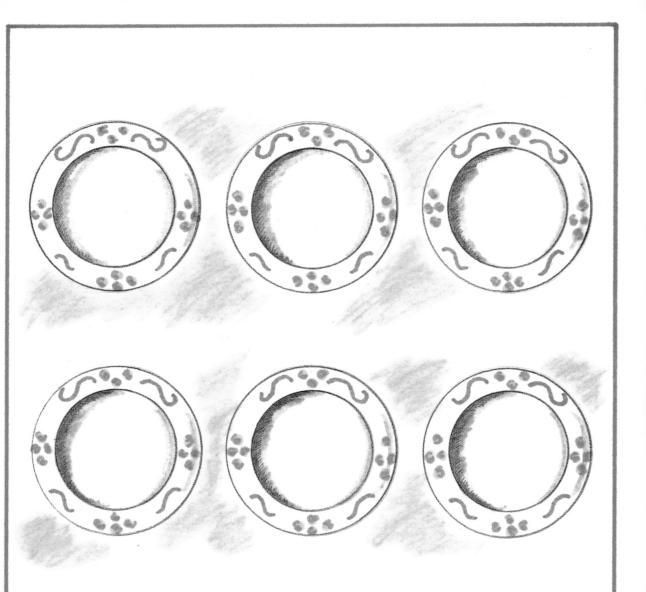

We put one out
For our Shabbos guest.

Seven fine forks
To use when we eat,

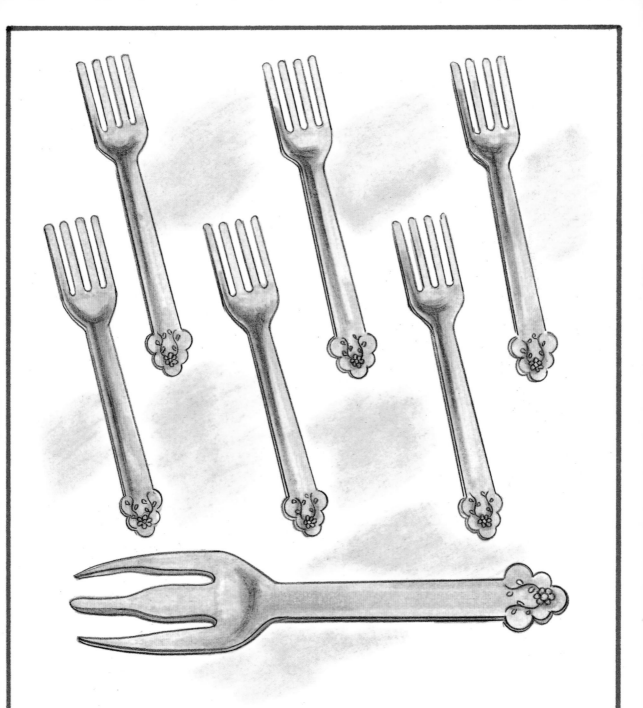

The biggest one is
For serving meat.

Eight silver spoons
For soup and for tea,

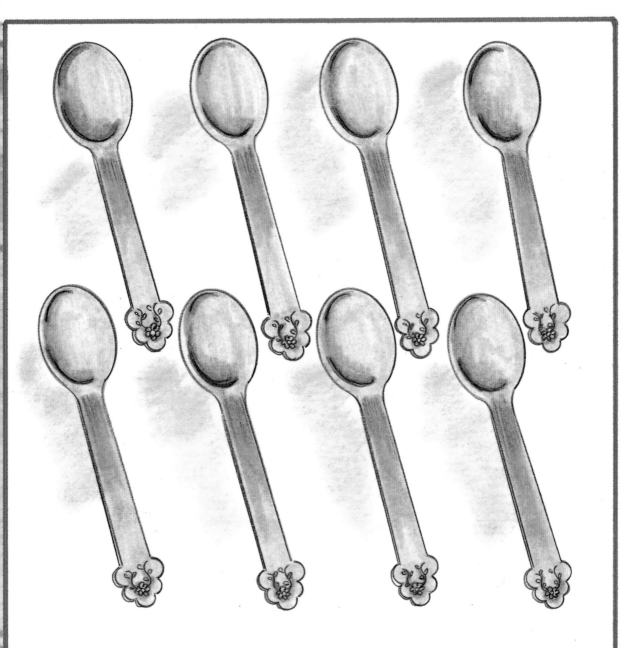

We set them on the table
As fast as can be.

9

Nine cookies for dessert,

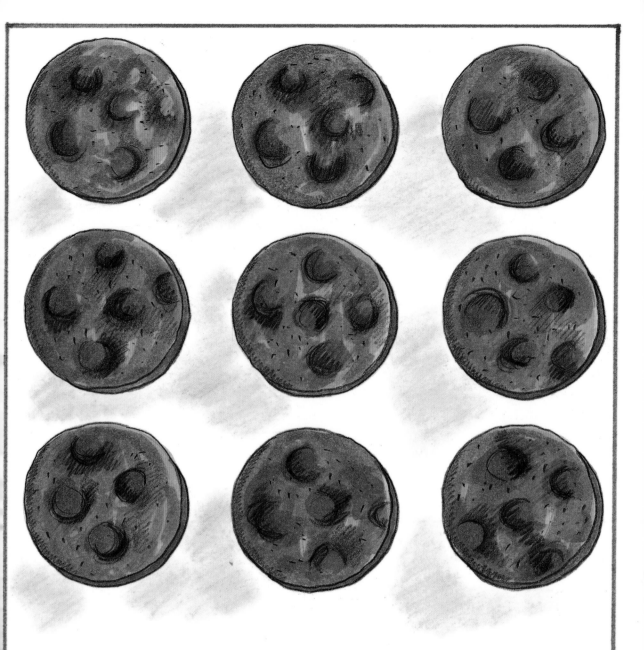

What a special treat!

And ten nice napkins

To help keep us neat.

The table is set,
We have counted to ten.
Next week, let's try it
Once again!

Shabbos candles are lit 18 minutes before sunset every Friday.

The brocha (blessing) is:

בָּרוּךְ אַתָּה ד׳ אֱ-לֹקֵינוּ מֶלֶךְ הָעוֹלָם
אֲשֶׁר קִדְּשָׁנוּ בְּמִצְוֹתָיו,
וְצִוָּנוּ לְהַדְלִיק נֵר שֶׁל שַׁבָּת קֹדֶשׁ

Bo-ruch A-toh Ado-noi E-lo-hei-nu Me-lech Ha-olom
A-sher Ki-de-sho-nu Be-mitz-vo-sov Vi-tzi-vo-nu
Le-had-lik Ner Shel Sha-bos Ko-desh.

GLOSSARY
Bentchers - booklets containing the Grace after Meals
Challos - Shabbos loaves
Hashem - G-d
Kiddush - blessing over wine recited on Shabbos and Festivals
Shabbos - Sabbath

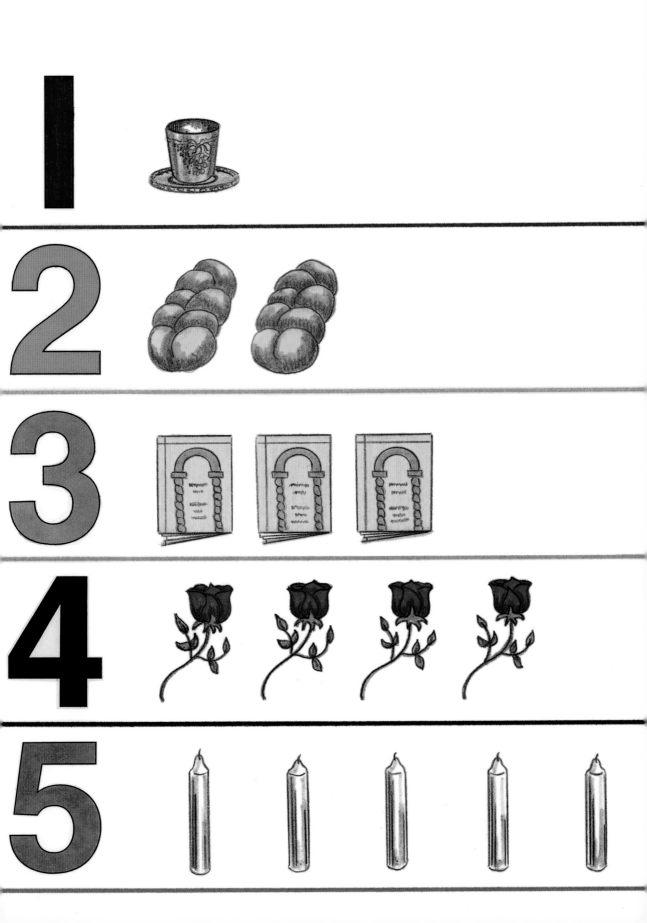

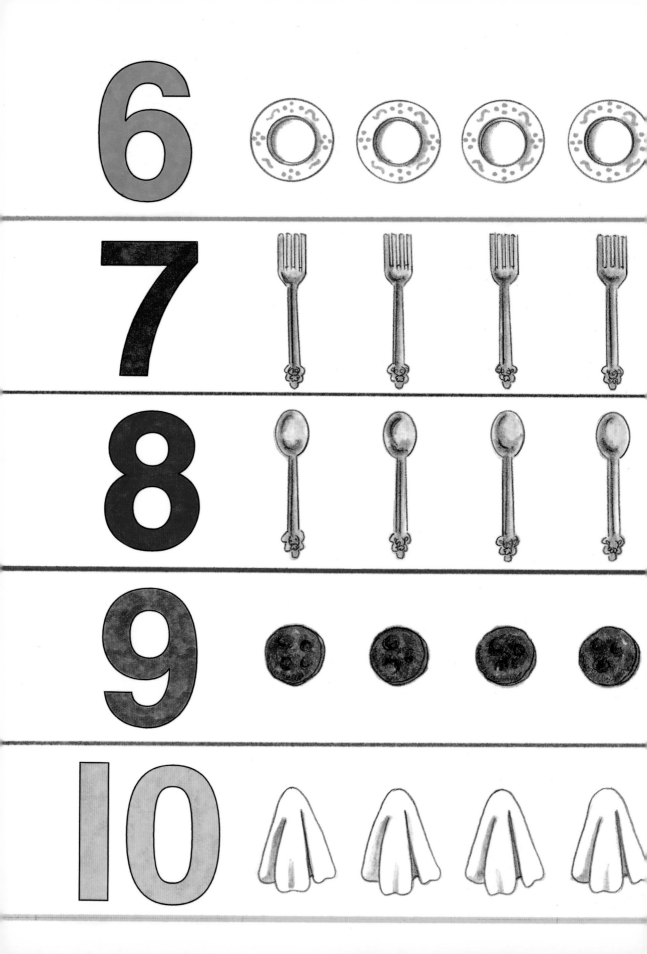

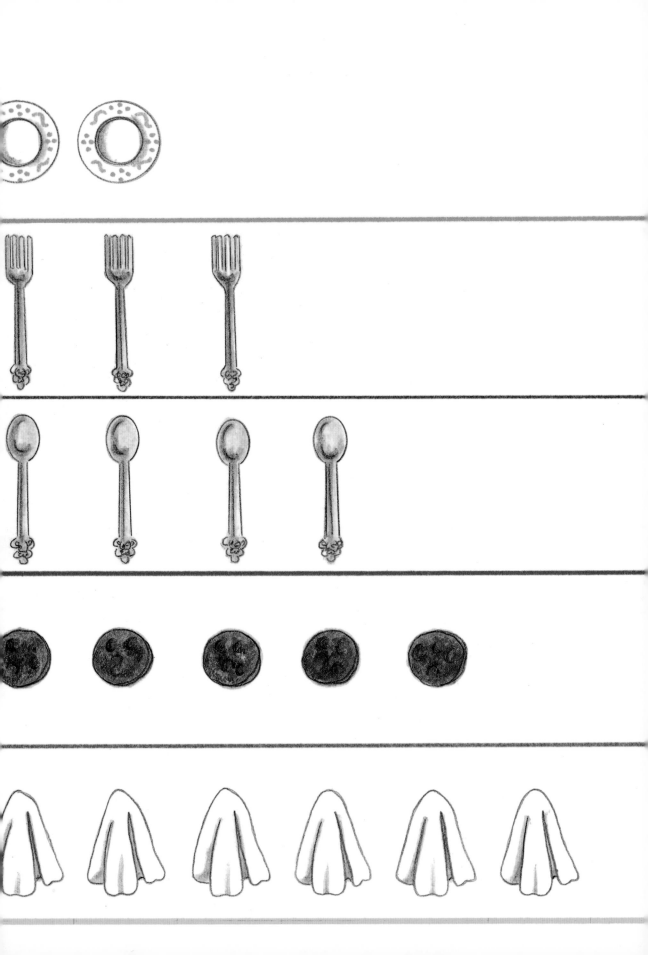